This library edition published in 2018 by Walter Foster Jr.,
an imprint of The Quarto Group
6 Orchard Road, Suite 100
Lake Forest, CA 92630

Distributed in the United States and Canada by
Lerner Publisher Services
241 First Avenue North
Minneapolis, MN 55401 U.S.A.
www.lernerbooks.com

First Library Edition

    Library of Congress Cataloging-in-Publication Data

Names: Hamscher, Cory, illustrator.
Title: Learn to draw Marvel's Guardians of the Galaxy / character art by
Cory Hamscher.
Description: Lake Forest, CA : Published by Walter Foster Jr., an imprint of
    The Quarto Group, 2017.
Identifiers: LCCN 2017035004 | ISBN 9781942875482 (hardcover)
Subjects: LCSH: Science fiction in art. | Drawing--Technique. | Guardians of
    the Galaxy (Motion picture)
Classification: LCC NC825.S34 L425 2017 | DDC 741.5/1--dc23
LC record available at https://lccn.loc.gov/2017035004

Printed in USA
9 8 7 6 5 4 3 2 1

TABLE OF CONTENTS

TOOLS & MATERIALS

You need to gather only a few simple art supplies before you begin. Start with a drawing pencil and an eraser. Make sure you also have a pencil sharpener and a ruler. To add color to your drawings, use markers, colored pencils, crayons, watercolors, or acrylic paint. The choice is yours!

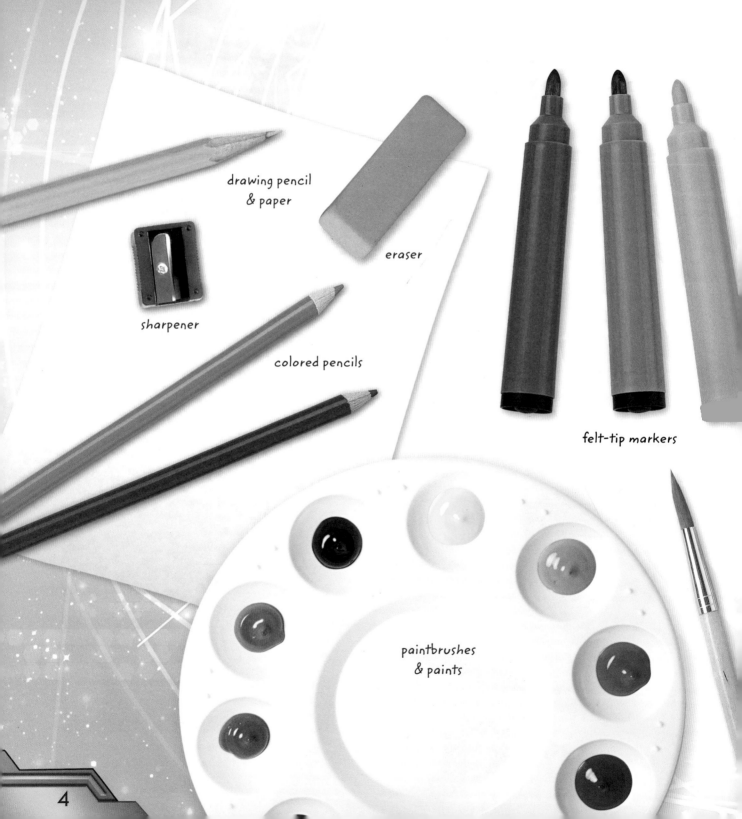

drawing pencil & paper

eraser

sharpener

colored pencils

felt-tip markers

paintbrushes & paints

Use tracing paper, which you can find at your local arts and crafts store, to trace the characters pictured.

tracing paper

Make sure the tracing paper is placed over the character you want to draw. You should be able to see through the tracing paper.

With your pencil, draw everything you can see over the character you're tracing.

Pay close attention to all the little details.

GRID METHOD DRAWING BASICS

When using the grid method, don't worry about the drawing as a whole. Focus on copying the lines and shapes of just one small square at a time.

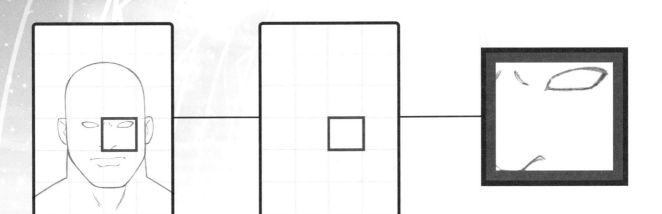

Choose a square and copy everything into the same square on your blank practice grid. Make sure you are copying the shapes and lines into the correct spot!

After you've completed all the squares in step one, move on to the next step and keep going! Add color, and you're done!

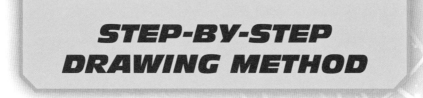

When using the step-by-step drawing method, you will begin by drawing very basic shapes, such as lines and circles.

1

First draw the basic shapes, using light lines that will be easy to erase.

2

Pay attention to the new lines added in each step.

3

Erase guidelines and add more detail.

4

In each new step, add more defining lines.

5

Take your time adding detail and copying what you see.

6

Add color to your drawing with colored pencils, markers, paints, or crayons!

STAR-LORD

A headstrong intergalactic adventurer, Peter Quill was taken from his home on Earth at a young age, growing up in outer space alongside the pirate-like Ravagers. As the intrepid Star-Lord, Quill travels the cosmos in his spaceship, the Milano, seeking his fortune. Equipped with a high-tech blaster and a mix-tape of music from home, Star-Lord leads an unlikely team of interstellar misfits—the Guardians of the Galaxy—in their attempts to do a little good, a little bad, a little of both!

Powers & Weapons

- Unique blaster that works only in his hands
- High-tech mask with a variety of vision modes
- Enhanced healing
- Personal energy shields
- Can see all energy spectra with cybernetic implant
- 100% memory recall
- Gifted strategist, thinks outside the box
- Skilled marksman and swordsman

USE TRACING
PAPER TO DRAW
STAR-LORD.

Copy the lines shown in each step. When you're done with all the steps, you'll have a completed drawing of Star-Lord. Color your drawing with markers, colored pencils, crayons, or paints.

STEP ONE

STEP TWO

STEP THREE

STEP FOUR

STEP FIVE

GRID METHOD

Follow along, first drawing basic shapes with light pencil lines. Copy the new lines shown in each step, eventually darkening the lines you want to keep and erasing the rest. Finally add color to your drawing with colored pencils, markers, paints, or crayons.

1

2

8

GAMORA

Orphaned as a child when the rest of her species was annihilated, Gamora was found and raised by the tyrant Thanos, who conditioned her to become an unparalleled warrior. Weary of the acts she was forced to commit in her adoptive father's name, Gamora later broke free of her chains. Teaming up with Star-Lord and his motley crew, the "most dangerous woman in the galaxy" now seeks to redeem her past crimes, putting her extraordinary skills to use as a member of the Guardians of the Galaxy.

Powers & Weapons

- Master of hand-to-hand combat
- Proficient in a wide variety of weaponry, including blasters and swords
- Highly skilled in the art of subterfuge
- Increased strength, agility, physical conditioning, and healing
- Cybernetic implants
- Genetic alteration

USE TRACING PAPER TO DRAW GAMORA.

Copy the lines shown in each step. When you're done with all the steps, you'll have a completed drawing of Gamora. Color your drawing with markers, colored pencils, crayons, or paints.

STEP ONE

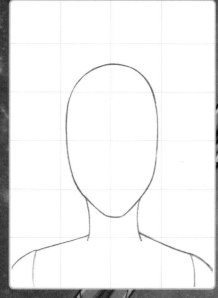

STEP TWO

STEP THREE

STEP FOUR

STEP FIVE

GRID METHOD

Follow along, first drawing basic shapes with light pencil lines. Copy the new lines shown in each step, eventually darkening the lines you want to keep and erasing the rest. Finally add color to your drawing with colored pencils, markers, paints, or crayons.

1

2

ROCKET

Though he may look like a common Earth raccoon, the temperamental Rocket is in fact a one-of-a-kind genetically produced being, originally created on the planet Halfworld. This diminutive, tough-talking creature is a master pilot, engineer, marksman, and weapons specialist. Previously a small-time thief along with his partner Groot, Rocket lends his genius and heavy artillery to the Guardians of the Galaxy, unable to resist the call of adventure (and plunder)!

Powers & Weapons

- Genetically and cybernetically enhanced
- Highly agile
- Mechanical genius, with particular aptitude in engineering, vehicles, and heavy munitions
- Intuitive ability to pilot most vehicles

USE TRACING
PAPER TO DRAW
ROCKET.

Copy the lines shown in each step. When you're done with all the steps, you'll have a completed drawing of Rocket. Color your drawing with markers, colored pencils, crayons, or paints.

STEP ONE

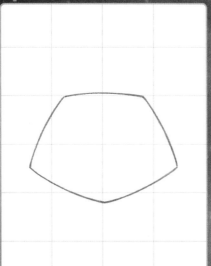

STEP TWO

STEP THREE

STEP FOUR

STEP FIVE

GRID METHOD

Follow along, first drawing basic shapes with light pencil lines. Copy the new lines shown in each step, eventually darkening the lines you want to keep and erasing the rest. Finally add color to your drawing with colored pencils, markers, paints, or crayons.

1

2

3

6

DRAX

Fueled by a personal vendetta against those who cost him his family, the rough-edged warrior called Drax the Destroyer has room in his life for little else besides revenge. To this end, the heavily tattooed Drax has long relied upon his proficiency in battle and his razor-sharp blades to do his talking for him. After making a tentative alliance with the Guardians of the Galaxy, the untamed Drax must learn to put the needs of the universe before his own.

Powers & Weapons

- Superhuman strength and durability
- Ferocious hand-to-hand combat
- Highly skilled with blades and other close combat gear

USE TRACING
PAPER TO DRAW
DRAX.

Copy the lines shown in each step. When you're done with all the steps, you'll have a completed drawing of Drax. Color your drawing with markers, colored pencils, crayons, or paints.

STEP ONE

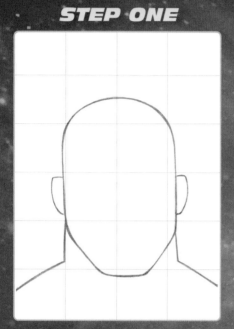

STEP TWO

STEP THREE

STEP FOUR

STEP FIVE

Follow along, first drawing basic shapes with light pencil lines. Copy the new lines shown in each step, eventually darkening the lines you want to keep and erasing the rest. Finally add color to your drawing with colored pencils, markers, paints, or crayons.

1

2

GROOT

The last surviving member of a tree-like alien race, Groot is perhaps one of the most unusual beings in all of the cosmos. Though calm and quiet in most instances, he is known to unleash his tremendous strength on an enemy foolish enough to threaten his allies, particularly his longtime partner in crime, Rocket. Though he can only vocalize using the phrase, "I am Groot," the gentle giant's friends are nevertheless able to understand his exact meaning through his subtle inflections.

Powers & Weapons

- Superhuman strength
- Ability to regenerate physical damage
- Plant-like form enables him to grow or reshape his limbs and root himself in place for enhanced stability
- Can emit glowing spores

USE TRACING
PAPER TO DRAW
GROOT.

Copy the lines shown in each step. When
you're done with all the steps, you'll have
a completed drawing of Groot. Color your
drawing with markers, colored pencils,
crayons, or paints.

STEP ONE

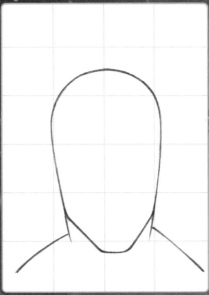

STEP TWO

STEP THREE

STEP FOUR

STEP FIVE

Follow along, first drawing basic shapes with light pencil lines. Copy the new lines shown in each step, eventually darkening the lines you want to keep and erasing the rest. Finally add color to your drawing with colored pencils, markers, paints, or crayons.

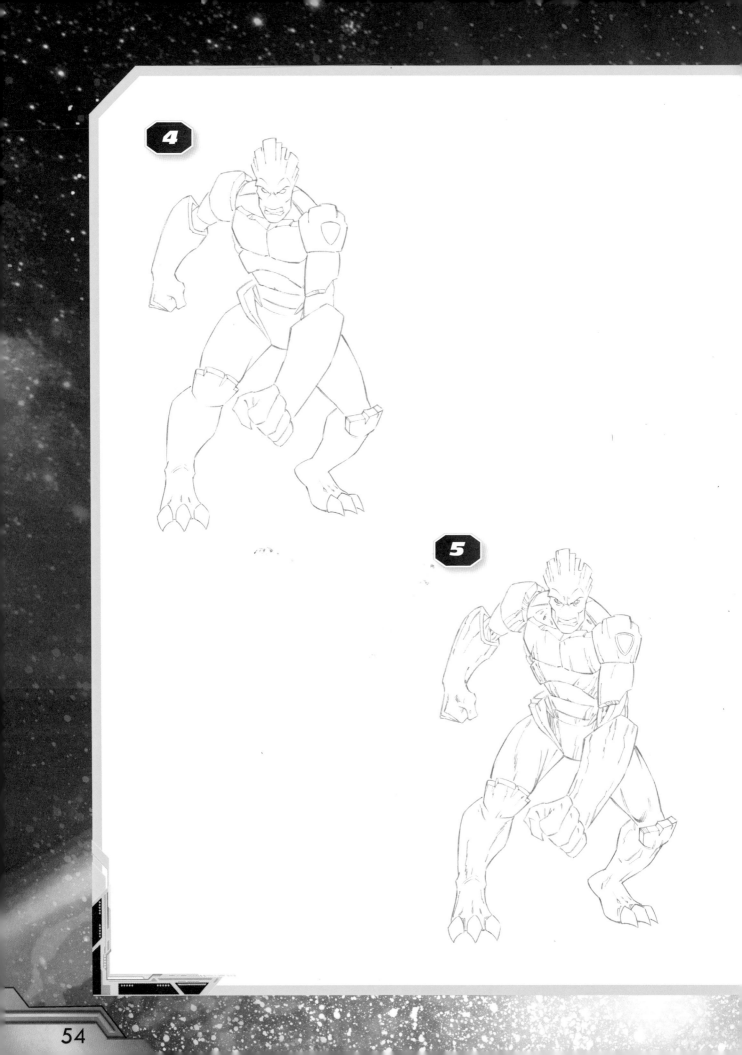

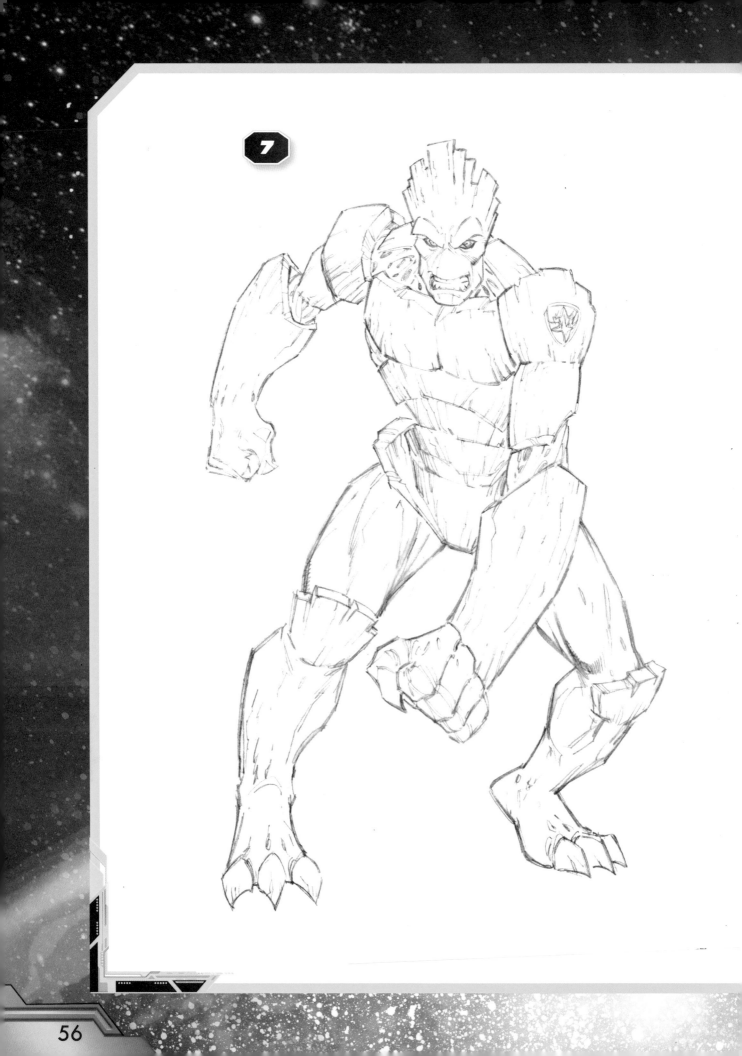

Copy the lines shown in each step. When you're done with all the steps, you'll have a completed drawing of young Groot. Color your drawing with markers, colored pencils, crayons, or paints.

STEP ONE

STEP TWO

GRID METHOD

STEP FIVE

Draw Peter Quill's trusty starship, the Milano, using the step-by-step method. Follow along, first drawing basic shapes with light pencil lines. Copy the new lines shown in each step, eventually darkening the lines you want to keep and erasing the rest. Finally add color to your drawing with colored pencils, markers, paints, or crayons.

1

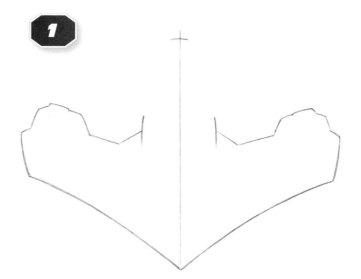

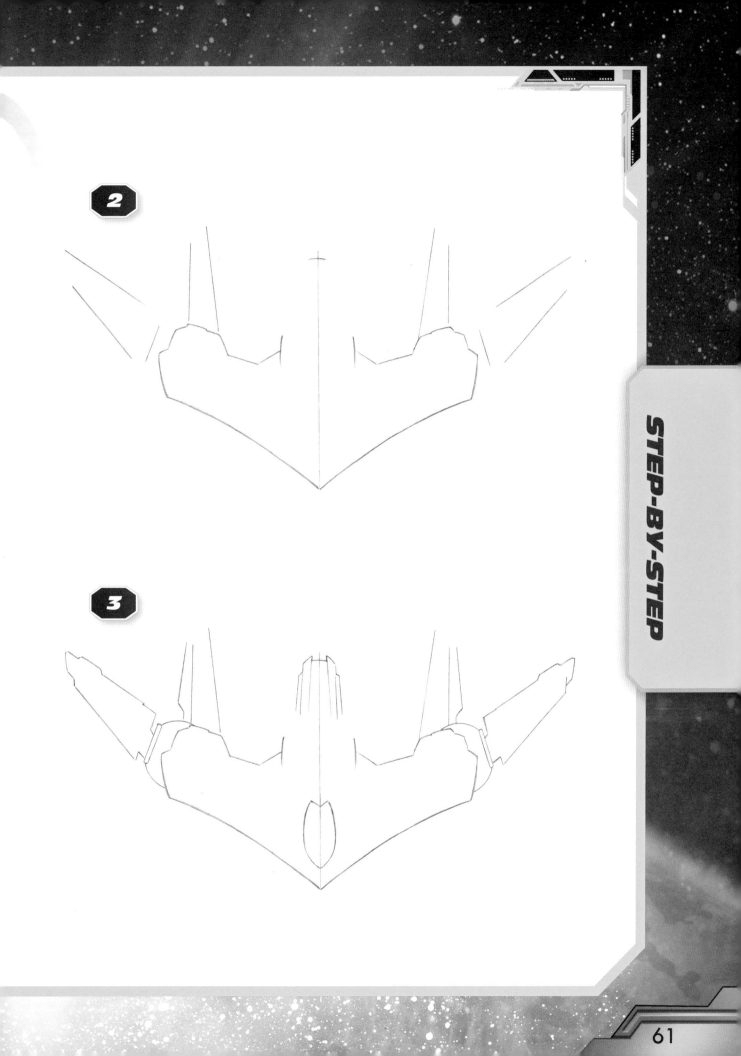

2

3

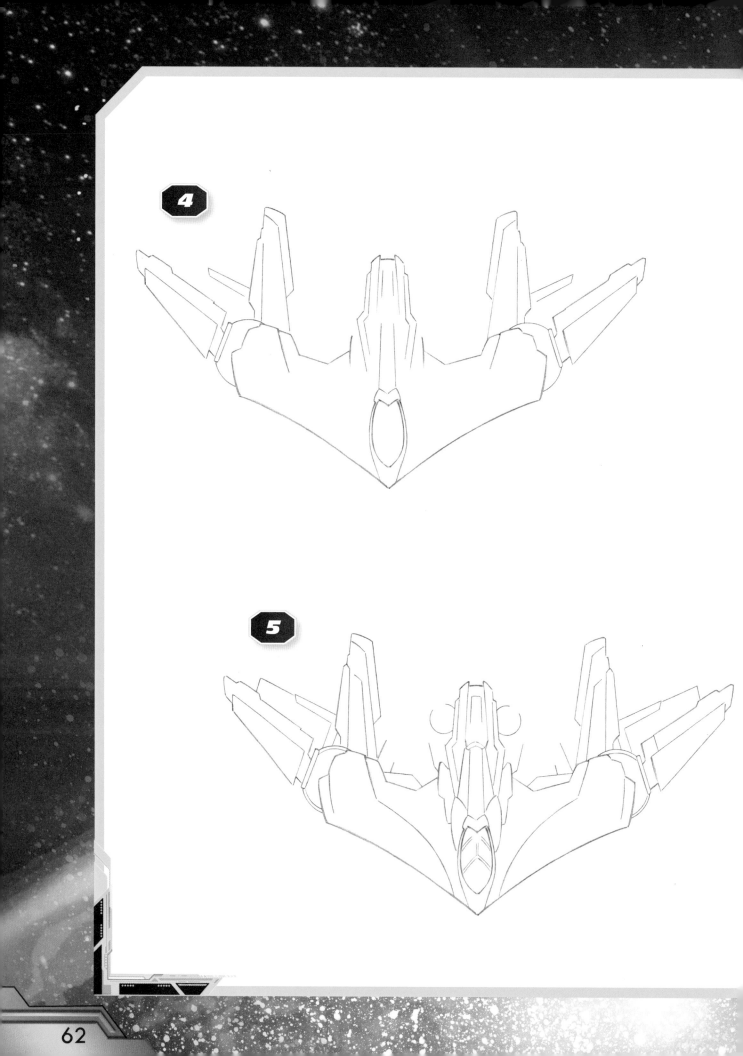

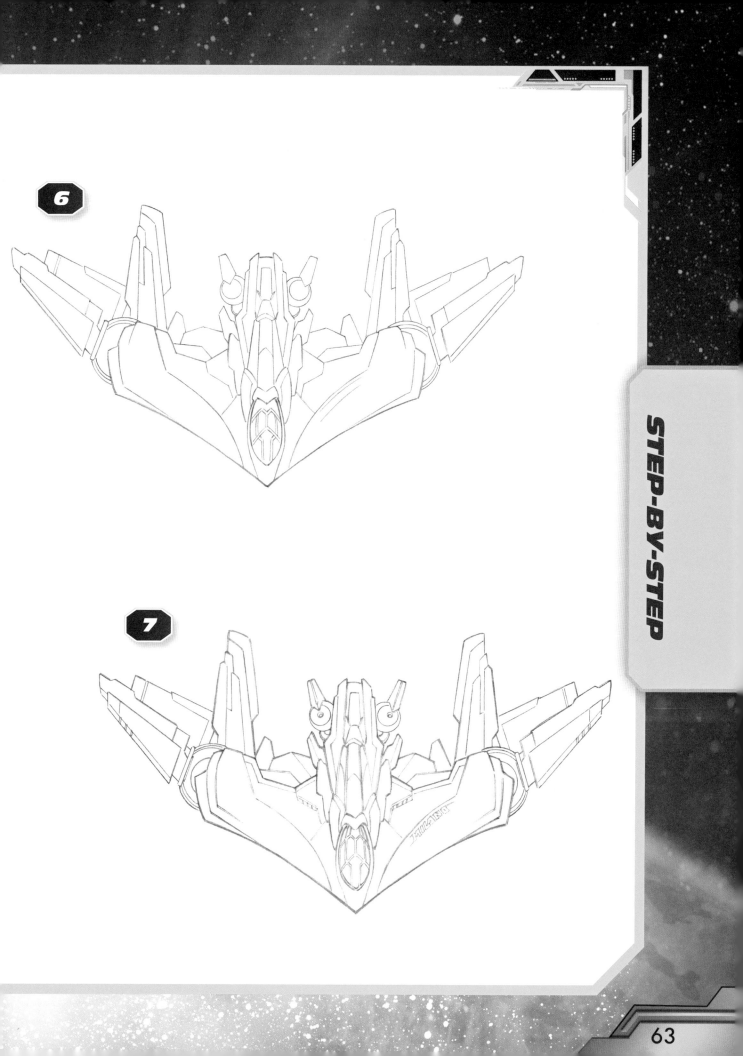